THE LAST DAY OF JESUS

THE LAST DAY OF JESUS

An Enriching Portrayal of the Passion

GERHARD LOHFINK

AVE MARIA PRESS   Notre Dame, Indiana

Translator's note: All biblical quotations in this English translation are from *The Jerusalem Bible*. The quotations from Flavius Josephus and from Philo of Alexandria are from the standard English editions of these classic authors.

Translated from the German by Salvator Attanasio

Originally published in German as *Der Letzte Tag Jesu* by Verlag Herder, Freiburg im Breisgau. © 1981

International Standard Book Number: 0-87793-312-X

Library of Congress Catalog Card Number: 83-73026

Cover design: Elizabeth French

Printed and bound in the United States of America.

For Elfriede and Walter Kirchner

CONTENTS

FOREWORD

The passion of Jesus was not a religious play, nor was the cross of Jesus the decorative image which Christian craftsmanship later made it out to be. If you listen regularly to the recital of Christ's passion in the Holy Week liturgy, you can, of course, visualize the passion as a religious drama with its figures gradually taking on the appearance of an icon. But this would be a misunderstanding. And so the task of the interpreter is precisely that of repeatedly countering misunderstanding with reality. Exegetes are forever enjoined to point out that Jesus' passion was an actuality, an extremely concrete event that unfolded amid the play of very real power blocs which successfully pursued their interests to the end with deadly earnestness.

Obviously, sceptics are ill equipped for this task. For their mistrust sees in everything only legends, literary compositions and symbolic meanings. Such interpretations cut the historical reality from underfoot and render the real happening of the passion almost inaccessible. In this way the scandalous and bloody death of Jesus on the cross is no longer a clear and intelligible reality.

In the following presentation, I would like

to avoid a result of this kind. I will follow the events of the passion, what really happened, completely in the light of critical gospel research but without that radical scepticism which entrusts the carefully transmitted and anxiously guarded laws of criticism more than the gospels themselves.

Our topic is intentionally limited; neither Jesus' Last Supper nor the Easter events are discussed, only those of the day on which Jesus died. But even much of what transpired on this one day is also left out of consideration. All the theological interpretations of the passion, in which the gospel's narration is extremely rich, are intentionally set aside. Thus the discussion of what really happened at that time is selective. Only an interpretation that unveils meaning in the light of faith can disclose the true dimension of the happening. This bias has been intentionally chosen. It should also be made clear that the presentation offered here cannot be viewed as an imitation or, even less, as a substitute for the passion narratives. All historical penetration of the passion, undertaken with believing eyes, ultimately and by necessity points to the gospels themselves, where the meaning of the events of that time is superbly and authoritatively disclosed to us.

—Gerhard Lohfink

1
THE CONFLICT

On a Friday more than 1,900 years ago (about April 7, 30 A.D.), Jesus of Nazareth was executed as a political criminal on a hill near the city of Jerusalem. The year of his death can no longer be established with absolute certainty. But an exact knowledge of the date is of minor importance. More important is the question of how it was possible for the condemnation and execution of Jesus to have occurred in the first place.

On this point we must clearly realize that in Jerusalem at the time a conflict that had already begun in Galilee reached a highly critical stage: Jesus encountered hostility soon after his first public appearance (cf. Mk 3:6), and this hostility steadily intensified.

It would, of course, be frivolous to speak simply of the Jews as his enemies. After all, Jesus himself was a Jew, and all his friends, followers and sympathizers were Jews. If Jesus' enemies are to be designated with greater precision, careful distinctions must be made among individual groups.

The hostile group most frequently mentioned in the gospels is the party or sect of the Pharisees. It was a very influential lay movement, which was organized in fellowships or communities (in Hebrew: *haburot*) and which had followers and settlements throughout the country. The leaders and the most important members of the pharisaic communities were scribes. Not all scribes by far were Pharisees. The sect had developed when, after the Maccabean war of liberation, the "liberators," though themselves Jews, had erected a lordship system that was at least as corrupt and as removed from Israel's true tradition as that of the preceding Jewish collaborators with the Greek foreign domination.

Thus, from the outset, the Pharisees were something of a conservative protest movement. Their conservatism, however, must not be viewed with too much bias. Beyond the Mosaic Law the Pharisees used the oral interpretation of tradition to make the old biblical prescriptions understood and practicable to the Jews of the time. In contrast to other Jewish groups, the Pharisees did not separate themselves from the people. Rather, they tried to educate them to a meaningful observance of the Law. Because they repeatedly protected the people against the arbitrary demands of the powerful, the Pharisees had them on their side and they, in turn, were held in high esteem. On the whole, their religious zeal was deep and genuine. Only on that basis are the harsh, verbal clashes with Jesus fully understandable.

In Jesus, therefore, the Pharisees en-
counter a man who is as deeply believing as
themselves yet who can set aside the tradition
of the Fathers, indeed even the Law of Moses if
need be, in order to inquire after the real will
of God. To be sure, a certain freedom in
regard to tradition also marks the Pharisees,
but they can comprehend the radical freedom
with which Jesus speaks and acts only as
outrageous arrogance and blasphemy. To
them the scripture and the interpretation of
scripture by the Fathers are all and everything.
But Jesus is concerned above all with the will
of God that announces itself then and there, in
the hour of his public life.

The limitation of the pharisaic movement
is made clear precisely on this point. It did, to
be sure, reckon with a future intercession of
God in history. But when the chips were
down, it was not in a position to grasp a wholly new future salvation that could burst the
frame of the old. The "kingship of God" would
be but a continuation, in a perfect form, of
what was already known to Israel in her Law.
Hence, according to the pharisaic conception,
to interpret God's will meant to consult the
whole Law and all the pronouncements of
earlier doctors of the Law. Jesus does nothing
of the sort. He comes forward with the claim

to proclaim God's will, freshly and definitively, without any scribal methodology. Nowhere is this shocking claim better expounded than in the contrasting statements of the Sermon on the Mount: "You have learned how it was said to our ancestors . . . But I say this to you . . ." (Mt 5:21-48). Even more, Jesus not only interprets the Law freshly and radically with a view to God's ultimate will but he advances the claim that he is already ushering in the new age of salvation by his words and his actions. What is most perplexing and disconcerting about this is the linking of the new to his own person and, most pointedly, not to the saving actions of God in the past. Jesus comes forward point-blank with the appalling claim that God's final salvation begins with his own actions.

This claim, linked to the comforting promise extended to sinners, makes the constant conflicts of Jesus with the Pharisees fully understandable. The extremists among them must have been deeply convinced that Jesus had to be eliminated for the sake of Israel's faith (cf. Mk 3:6). Jesus' transgressions against the Law and tradition made him appear as one leading the people astray (Mt 27:63; Jn 7:12, 47). And he was bound to be viewed as a blasphemer when he spoke and acted as though he himself would stand in God's place.

According to the Mosaic Law (cf. Dt 13: 2-12) and its scribal interpretation, tempters and blasphemers were to be killed. Thus Jesus' enemies among the Pharisees must also have been convinced that by entertaining such an intent they were doing God a service. One does them an injustice and minimizes their conflict with Jesus if one imputes other motives to them.

A second group which confronted Jesus, especially in Jerusalem, was the Sadducees. Their orientation reflected the interests and concerns of the wealthy upper-class and, above all, the priestly aristocracy. This is why the Sadducees are always at issue when the gospels mention the high priests. The Sadducees had constituted the ruling elite since the return of Israel from the exile. For a time they had been entirely dislodged from their position by the Hasmoneans and Herodians. In contrast to the Pharisees, they rejected an extension of the Law through oral tradition. Only the letter of the Mosaic Law was authoritative for them. In other respects they permitted all that struck them as significant—even strong cultural influences from the Hellenist-Roman world. They most rigorously objected to apocalyptic expectations, and cultic-ritual concerns wholly occupied the center of their religious practice.

At the time of Jesus the high priest was not only the spiritual head of the Jews but, by order of the Roman occupying power, he was also responsible for the territorial administration of the province of Judaea. Thus the Sadducees had experience with the exercise of power and with the practice of politics. Obviously they wanted to avoid any disturbance of the delicate political situation of Judaea, for this would endanger the last remnant of Jewish freedom. They undoubtedly believed that Jesus and his followers should not be allowed to spread their message because something could erupt which at any moment would drive the Romans to undertake reprisals against Jewish self-rule.

To be sure, religious reasons also played a decisive role in their hostility to Jesus. His apocalyptic message endangered their static, institutional thinking. But, above all, the factor that most deeply determined their position was Jesus' criticism of Temple practices. In a situation that is no longer reconstructible, Jesus must have openly taken a position against the Sadducean-priestly Temple ideology. Certainly he spoke through a prophetically barbed utterance about the final destruction of the Temple, but also of its miraculous new foundation by God. He might have expressed a prediction such as the following: "This Temple will be destroyed and in three days again be rebuilt" (cf. Mk 13:2 f.; Jn 2:19). In connection with this provocative utterance there certainly followed a prophetic symbolic action, the so-called cleansing of the Temple (cf. Mk 11:15-19, 27 f.). By so acting Jesus called into question what for the Sadducees was absolutely the central institution which guaranteed the country's welfare.

The members of a third group that assumed a hostile stance to Jesus are called Herodians in the gospels (Mk 3:6; 12:13). They were the followers and the minions of the Herodian ruling house. Herod Antipas, a son of Herod the Great, ruled in Galilee and Perea at the time of Jesus' public life. Herod the Great had also governed Judaea. Now, however, his family had been pushed back to the border regions by the Romans. The partisans of the dynasty, however, not only sat in Galilee and in East Jordan but unquestionably in Jerusalem as well (cf. Mk 12:13), awaiting their hour to strike. Their hostility to Jesus might have had political grounds. They must have found any movement that could become a popular religious movement eminently undesirable. In their view such an eventuality would only make the already complicated Jewish situation all the more strained and difficult and lessen their chances of seizing power.

Jesus, of course, did not have only enemies. A part of the people, above all in Galilee, openly sided with him. This overt partisanship even extended to the ranks of the groups hostile to him. In Mark 12:28-34, a conversation with a scribe is portrayed positively. Jesus also had sympathizers in Jerusalem as is shown by the example of Joseph of Arimathaea (Mk 15:43) and the development of the primitive community after Easter. Above all, a circle of followers and disciples gathered around him and accompanied him on his wanderings.

We would very much like to know the attitude of the Essenes toward Jesus, those people about whom we have more exact knowledge today than did earlier generations of researchers thanks to the discovery of the Dead Sea Scrolls at Qumran. The Essenes, like Jesus, desired the apocalyptic gathering and renewal of Israel. To be sure, they sought to achieve this—in utter contrast to Jesus—by withdrawing into their community and by considering it as a sacred sphere where alone cultic purity was possible. Strikingly, no report of a single conflict between Jesus and the Essenes has come down to us. Their community is not mentioned even once in the gospels. Had they, like the majority of the Pharisees, rejected Jesus? Or had they looked upon his public ministry, despite all the differences between them and him, with a certain sympathy?

When one poses the question seeking to determine the grounds that led Jesus to his death, the discussion, in any event, may not be limited to the Pharisees, the Sadducees, the high priests and the Herodians. That Jesus ended on the cross was an event also occasioned by the indifference of many who did not concern themselves at all with his message. And it was also brought about by the wait-and-see attitude of those who did not want to come to a quick decision. For Jesus' message was bound to lead Israel into a deep crisis. It demanded a radical decision. Those who did not decide, or indefinitely postponed their decision, decided willy-nilly against Jesus. Obviously, viewed on the whole, Jesus had not found sufficient credence. His enemies, therefore, could direct events in their own way in accord with their inclinations.

2
THE DEATH SENTENCE

We do not know exactly when it was decided that Jesus had to be executed. The situation had become extremely tense just before the last Passover feast when Jesus had set out for Jerusalem. As already indicated, the last straw most probably was the cleansing of the Temple and Jesus' prophecy regarding the Temple. In Jerusalem one was particularly sensitive about matters concerning the Temple, for the Temple was not only the great religious symbol of Israel, it also ensured the city's economic and social power.

In Mark 14:1-2 it is reported that the chief priests and the scribes were looking for a possible way to get their hands on Jesus in order to put him to death. At the same time, of course, they were of the opinion that it must not be during the festivities, or there would be a disturbance among the people. Hence Jesus was not to be seized in public, in the crowd of pilgrims. His arrest was to be carried out without attracting the slightest attention because his foes took due account of the people's sympathetic attitudes toward him. Above all they did not want to stir up the Galileans and the plain rural folk.

Unquestionably, this had all been realistically thought out in advance. Vast multitudes of pilgrims poured into the Holy City for the Passover festival, and among them there surely were many people who knew Jesus and judged him favorably. Moreover, it was precisely during the festival of Passover that apocalyptic expectations buoyantly soared with new fervor. For this reason, from the viewpoint of the Jewish authorities, it was eminently logical to want to undertake the arrest of Jesus in absolute secrecy and with no public stir. That Judas Iscariot, a man from the circle of the Twelve, offered his cooperation for a smooth, friction-free arrest must have been most welcome to the leadership.

One might ask, just what, precisely, did Judas' "betrayal" consist in? Basically, he provided information to the Jewish authorities about a suitable place and a suitable time for making the arrest. There has been much puzzlement about Judas' motives for his betrayal. The early Christian legend, whose proliferations already begin in the New Testament, imputed to him ordinary and primitive greed for money (cf. Mt 26:14-16; Jn 12:6). Many exegetes, however, are not satisfied with this explanation. For a time a popular interpretation held that Judas entertained exaggerated national and messianic expectations and was subsequently deeply disenchanted with Jesus and for this reason decided to betray him. This, however, remains pure speculation, as unprovable as Judas' alleged greed. We must simply content ourselves with the information that the betrayer was one of the Twelve and that he belonged to the select circle of the disciples. Jesus most certainly was not spared any of the deviltries that customarily unfold among human beings.

3
THE ARREST

During the night, between Thursday and Friday, Jesus was arrested in the region of the Mount of Olives, hence east of Jerusalem, on a site that was known as Gethsemane. There is no ground whatsoever for considering the entire arrest scene, narrated in Mark, as unhistorical. The Judas kiss, in particular, is viewed by some critical researchers as indicating a legendary story-motif. Contrary to this view, it can be pointed out that the arrest takes place at night and a clear sign was needed. After several unsuccessful attempts, as reported in the Johannine gospel (cf. 7:30,32,44; 10:39), this time Jesus' enemies wanted to be absolutely sure they got their hands on him.

In Mark we read: "Even while he was speaking, Judas, one of the Twelve, came up with a number of men armed with swords and clubs, sent by the chief priests and the scribes and the elders" (Mk 14:43). That sounds as though it might have involved an improvised squad, if not, indeed, a mercenary rabble. The Bible translators should have written of "billies" or truncheons, however, rather than swords and clubs, for the former is precisely what is meant. It then becomes clear that a police squad or detail was involved.

Obviously, in addition to the Temple guard, the Council had at its disposal a police detachment for necessary preservation of order, for making arrests and for the custody of prisoners. It clearly follows then that it is an official arrest by the Council that unfolds here completely within the framework of normal procedure. A greater number of armed men had been dispatched to the site because of the disciples who, the authorities knew, were with Jesus at the time.

Obviously the disciples are utterly surprised by the sudden arrest of Jesus. They flee and leave Jesus in the lurch.

Jesus is led back to the city across the Kedron Valley. According to the report in the Markan gospel, he is immediately brought to the house of the officiating high priest, where the members of the Council then come together for a night session in order to sit in judgment on him (Mk 14:53).

The description in the Johannine gospel differs quite markedly from this presentation. According to the fourth gospel, Jesus is first of all led to the former high priest, Annas, who subjected him to a kind of "pre-trial hearing" and only then was he brought before the officiating high priest, Caiaphas (Jn 18:12-24). No subsequent Council session is portrayed in the Johannine gospel.

Thus in the context of the fourth gospel, the hearing before Annas takes the place of the Council session noted by Mark. For this reason many exegetes assume that the Johannine description of Jesus' hearing before the high priest Annas, read according to the principles of the history of tradition, ultimately is based upon the same happening that Mark depicts as Jesus' hearing before the high priest Caiaphas, whose name is not mentioned in the Markan gospel. In the event that this assumption is correct, the Johannine presentation as regards this point must be considered only with the greatest caution in the reconstruction of the historical course of events. Yet it is certainly improbable that Jesus was arraigned before a Council without a pre-hearing and without, at least, the attempt to force from him damaging statements for presentation at the impending session. Moreover, the experienced former high priest, Annas, must have played an important role. But because of the difficulties the Johannine gospel presents when studied in the light of the history of tradition, one can at best conjecture all this. According to Mark's presentation, Jesus is simply brought to the house of the officiating high priest and there, in the middle of the night, the session of the Council begins.

4

THE COUNCIL'S NIGHT SESSION

In itself, holding a Council session during the night strikes one as strange. However, perhaps the situation does not appear so strange when one considers that the Jewish authorities, because of the gravity of the charges that they laid against Jesus, were allowed, indeed were required to hold an extraordinary court session. Besides, the Council was under the greatest pressure in terms of time because of the Passover feast. If one follows the Johannine narrative in particular, the day of the death of Jesus was the 14th of Nisan, Passover Preparation Day (Jn 19:14), and the slaughter of the Paschal lambs would have already started taking place in the afternoon in the Temple. The very acceptance of this chronology attests to the time pressure. If, however, one follows the synoptic chronology, Jesus died on the 15th of Nisan, hence on the very day of the Passover feast. In that case the time pressure would have been all the greater, because the holding of a Jewish court session in the light of day on Passover simply had to be avoided by all means.

Whether you consider the Johannine or the synoptic chronology as primary, you must realize that the Council had placed itself under enormous time pressure by ordering the arrest of Jesus within an extremely limited time span. From its perspective, to wait until after the feast was completely out of the question. After all, Jesus' arrest could not remain hidden for too long, and it was feared that his sympathizers among the people would be organized. So the authorities acted swiftly and decisively: The Council met in a night session.

In Mark 14:53 we read: "They led Jesus off to the high priest; and all the chief priests and the elders and the scribes assembled there." Thereby Mark precisely names the three groups, numbering 71 people, which composed the Council or Sanhedrin.

To the first group belonged the officiating high priests and the incumbents of a series of important Temple offices as, for example, the Temple head. In addition, it consisted of all the former high priests.

The second group consisted of the Elders. They came from the country's most influential lay families. Both the first and the second group were predominantly Sadducean in orientation.

The third faction of the Council was formed exclusively of the representatives of the order of scribes. And it was primarily in this group that the Pharisees had their spokesmen. Since the Council had judicial authority as well as being an administrative body, and since its judicial rulings were also religious rulings that needed an educated reading, the scribes in the Council possessed an important influence.

The only participant in the session whose name we know is Caiaphas, the officiating high priest (Mt 26:3; Jn 18:24). He must have been a resourceful diplomat and a very pragmatically oriented politician inasmuch as he managed to remain in power from 18 to 37 A.D. No other high priest in the first century had achieved a term of office stretching over 19 years. At that time, a high priest's term averaged four years. Caiaphas could never have maintained his position for so long if he had not had a powerful coterie behind the scenes and if he had not taken a flexible position toward the Roman procurator. Thus Caiaphas presides at that night session of the Council.

Mark writes that witnesses against Jesus stood up at the session, an observation that accords with Jewish court rules and proceedings of that time. For, in contrast to Roman trial proceedings in which the interrogation of the accused was the central point, in Jewish trial proceedings defense and prosecution witnesses were the focus. Witnesses for the prosecution,

in fact, performed the role of the public pros-
ecutor. The depositions of the witnesses had to
agree in every detail, no matter how minor,
otherwise they were deemed worthless and ir-
relevant for the continuation of the trial. Mark
says nothing about whether defense witnesses
in favor of Jesus stood up at the hearing.

What is of much greater importance to us,
of course, is the question of just what charge
Jesus stood under and on the basis of what
evidence was he ultimately condemned. Some
refer to the fact that he was accused of "leading
the people astray." A corresponding charge
had already been directed at Jesus during his
public activity (cf. Jn 7:12), and long after
Jesus' death we come upon this same charge in
Jewish sources: "Jesus has seduced and led
astray and alienated the affections of Israel,"
we read in the Babylonian Talmud (Sota 47a).
In particular those making the charge of
"leading astray" no doubt were thinking of
evidence such as disrespect of the Law and actions directed against the Temple. Both items
of evidence could even be interpreted as
blasphemy. Apparently, however, it was not
at all easy for the Council to juridically convict
Jesus beyond any question of doubt. Mark
(14:55-59) reports that the prosecution
witnesses did not agree, in consequence of
which the trial came to a standstill.

5
THE CHRIST CONFESSION

In this situation Caiaphas opened a new phase of the hearing by having Jesus arraigned before the court. Contrary to the simple presentation in Mark, we may on no account imagine Jesus as being present at the preceding interrogation of witnesses.

Jesus was only then led into the court-room, knowing nothing of the upshot of the hearing of witnesses. When the depositions of the prosecution witnesses were summarized for him, he said nothing and made no reply to questions (Mk 14:69 f.). Possibly the court, remembering the lack of agreement among the prosecution witnesses, came to real grief for lack of evidence because of Jesus' silence. And all this may have induced the high priest to take an extreme step that would force a verdict. Caiaphas asked Jesus: "Are you the Christ . . . the Son of the Blessed One?"

Nothing of a historical character contradicts the assertion that the high priest posed this question at that time. The question is significant, suggestive and plausible. It seizes upon opinions and rumors concerning Jesus that had been circulating a long time. In the last analysis, it raises the question of Jesus' authority with a quite definite understanding and within the horizon of a quite definite Jewish expectation.

The question of his authority had already been officially posed, and indeed by a delegation of the Council, soon after the incident in the Temple (Mk 11:27-33). At that time, Jesus had made no reply to them but had formulated a counter-question: "John's baptism, did it come from heaven, or from man?" Jesus' question obviously proceeded from the consideration that a public avowal is not opportune in every situation. The fact that the members of the delegation dodged the question and did not want to commit themselves proved Jesus' reserve to be correct in subsequent situations of this kind.

A few days later Jesus is again asked about his authority, now, of course, in a new situation. Now Jesus stands before the assembled Council, the country's primary religious court, and before the high priest, the representative of Israel. For a long time Jesus must have had a clear understanding of the definitive character of this moment. So now he answers directly, and in response to the question of whether he is the Christ, he confesses: "I am." And since he knows the misunderstandings to which the word "Christ" can give rise (cf. Mk 8:30), he interprets the Christ assertion immediately by the Son-of-Man assertion: He is the Christ, insofar as he is the Son of Man. He will soon be seated at the right hand of God and, as the apocalyptic judge himself, judge the Council that now sits in judgment on him: "And you will see the Son of Man seated at the right hand of the Power and coming with the clouds of heaven" (Mk 14:62).

Thereby Jesus makes clear his absolute authority—the same authority which had always been hidden in his words and deeds, an authority that goes far beyond all messianic and, especially, beyond all nationalistic messianic expectations. Threateningly, and as a testimony against them, he pronounces a last warning to his judges. It is the Council now that truly is in crisis and that is itself being put on trial.

Precisely because of its compelling drama, the scene between Jesus and Caiaphas has been designated by most critical exegesis as a fictional scene in which the post-Easter church with the help of Old Testament texts (Ps 110:1; Dan 7:13) asserted its own confession of faith in Jesus as the Christ and the Son of Man. What is certainly correct is that the confession of faith in Christ was a concern of the highest priority to the evangelists. Therefore, you have to realize that Caiaphas' question and Jesus' answer were already stylized in the light of primitive Christian theology. But even with this insight, the non-historic character of the happening as related is far from proved.

One thing, above all, must give us food for thought: As we shall see, Jesus was accused before Pilate of passing himself off as the Christ-king. It is precisely this point that proves decisive in the Roman proceedings against Jesus. To really understand this we should note that the Jewish charge could directly refer to his messianic confession before the Council and did not need to be substantiated by the actions of Jesus that might be interpreted as messianic. Those who quibble over Jesus' confession as the Christ before Caiaphas actually render the course of the passion events and the meshing of the two trials less plausible. It is advisable, therefore, to accord one's trust here, as well as in many other passages, to Mark's report. Jesus had made a messianic confession before the Council; he immediately defined it and surpassed it with the help of the Son-of-Man assertion.

With this confession which is also a prophetic threat against the Jewish court, Jesus now has forced the high priest to make a final decision. Now only two possibilities are open to the high priest: either belief in Jesus' claim to be the Son of Man or the conviction that he has heard an appalling blasphemy. The high priest's decision is unequivocal. For him, Jesus' confession that he is soon to appear as judge at the right hand of God is a shocking, blasphemous presumption. Now what one could rightly suspect for some time is firmly substantiated in the presence of many witnesses: Jesus is a false prophet, a tempter, a blasphemer.

Therefore, Caiaphas immediately does what the Law prescribes to anyone who has heard a blasphemy: He tears his robes. And he sets in motion what the Law prescribes in regard to a false prophet: He must be put to death; Israel must banish evil from its midst (cf. Dt 13:2-6). The rest of the Council concurs with Caiaphas' ruling. "And they all gave their verdict: he deserved to die" (Mk 14:64). Viewed juridically, it means that the Council establishes that Jesus has made himself guilty of a crime deserving death.

Immediately after this establishment of guilt there ensues a painful scene, barely believable, on the part of a supreme judicial authority. Some members of the Council spit on Jesus, blindfold him, strike him in the face and then demand that he prophesy (Mk 14:65). What is meant is that Jesus identify by name those who struck him.

Historical criticism has also announced its doubt in regard to this scene. Most critics assert that the mockery of Jesus most probably took place not before the Council, but at another site of the passion event. Certainly later tradition-history links the scene with the hearing before the Council. Jewish researchers, above all, have suggested that it be borne in mind that an incident of this kind could not conceivably have unfolded in front of the highest Jerusalem authority.

It is worth noting, however, that occurrences which today strike us as crude and as gross acts of lawlessness were in the ancient world often judged quite differently. Thus, for example, the tract *Sanhedrin* in the Babylonian Talmud states: "If someone strikes or insults one who is being led to his execution, he remains exempt from punishment, since the former has already incurred the death penalty anyway" (Sanh. 85a).

Moreover, it is precisely the mockery scene in Mark 14:65 that internally is closely coupled with the trial before the Council. For Jesus is indeed mocked as a false prophet. This ridicule certainly can be interpreted only as an embittered reaction to Jesus' prophetic threat that soon he himself would be the judge of his judges.

6

JESUS' DELIVERY TO PILATE

In connection with the mockery and mistreatment of Jesus, Mark relates the story of Peter's denial which must have taken place in the courtyard of the palace of the high priests. And he reports further of the drawing up of a formal decree for delivering Jesus to Pilate: "First thing in the morning, the chief priests together with the elders and scribes, in short the whole Sanhedrin, had their plan ready. They had Jesus bound and took him away and handed him over to Pilate" (Mk 15:1).

A new trial began immediately before Pilate, this time according to Roman law and under Roman chairmanship. The flawless meshing of the trial machinery was possible only because the Roman procurator, who otherwise resided in Caesarea on the coast, was sojourning in Jerusalem on account of the Passover feast. Also it was customary for the Romans to begin their judicial sessions very early in the morning, immediately after sunrise.

Now, naturally, we pose a whole series of questions to ourselves. Why two trials, and how did it come to that? Why a Roman trial after one had just taken place before Jewish legal authorities? And, conversely, if it was already known that a Roman trial procedure was required, why then did a Jewish trial unfold in the night? Further, just what kind of decree had been drawn up by the Council? Was it solely a bill of indictment or a formal death sentence?

The whole situation becomes comprehensible if we suppose with the majority of exegetes and with John 18:31 that the Roman occupying power at that time had stripped the Jews of jurisdiction in cases involving capital offenses.

This means that they no longer had the right to carry out a formal death sentence and, according to some exegetes, not even the right to pronounce a formal death sentence. The only exception allowed in the Roman regulation was an unauthorized entry into the Temple. If the Jews at that time had had the right to execute Jesus according to their own legal system, he would not have been crucified, but stoned to death. For crucifixion, though widespread in the ancient world, was especially characteristic of the Romans. It was practiced by the Jews only in a very few exceptional situations.

The fact that the Jewish authorities delivered Jesus to Pilate clearly shows that they viewed him as one convicted of a capital crime which in their opinion was punishable only with death. But in this case they have to waive their rights; it is incumbent upon the Roman procurator alone to inquire into the guilt of the accused and then to pass sentence according to Roman law.

The formal decree which the Council drew up as the night drew to a close must have been so formulated that it established Jesus' guilt and ordered his conviction. It is obvious that Pilate could not avoid the trial that was to evolve. By this means the Council members most certainly exerted pressure on him.

The decree they drafted, however, must have had another meaning: The Council members could justify to themselves the way in which they had pursued the matter of the charge against Jesus before the Roman procurator. After holding their own guilt-establishing trial, they could say that Jesus after all was a criminal deserving the death sentence, even though his condemnation by Pilate would be achieved only by the most questionable methods. We must now discuss these methods in the charge that was laid before Pilate.

The Council had condemned Jesus for blasphemy or, more exactly, it had established the factual evidence of blasphemy. Most probably the allegation that Jesus was leading the

people astray also played an important role.
Both were capital offenses within the Jewish
legal system. On the other hand, the charges of
blasphemy and of leading the people astray
made against a Jew before a Roman court were
viewed as religious transgressions concerning
exclusively the Jews. No Roman judge could
sentence a Jew to death for an infraction of
purely inner-Jewish religious laws. In the face
of such a charge, Pilate easily could have
spoken as did the proconsul Gallio years later
in Corinth: "Listen, you Jews. If this were a
misdemeanor or a crime, I would not hesitate
to attend to you; but if it is only quibbles
about words and names, and about your own
Law, then you must deal with it yourselves—I
have no intention of making legal decisions
about things like that" (Acts 18:14 f.).

The Council sees very clearly on this
point. Therefore, in a highly questionable
strategy, it brings the "Jesus case" before the
Romans under a different aspect: It makes a
political agitator out of "the seducer of the
people." It reverts to Jesus' confession as the
Christ and accuses him of being a false Christ
with political designs. Only thus can Pilate's
ironic question, "Are you King of the Jews?"
(Mk 15:2) be understood. Only thus can it be
fully grasped. And only thus can we comprehend why Jesus is executed with the inscrip-

tion, "The King of the Jews" (Mk 15:26) fixed
to his cross.

The charge that Jesus passed himself off as
Christ-king was so effective because at the
time of the Roman occupation of Palestine
almost every messianic movement was inevitably suspected of preparing a national
uprising against the Romans. "Christ-king"
indeed was almost synonymous with "free-
dom-fighter" and "political agitator"—and the
Romans were accustomed to react very swiftly, ruthlessly and effectively to the key word
"revolt." Here, moreover, lies one of the
reasons why Jesus during his public life ex-
hibited great reserve concerning the title of
Messiah.

If he was accused before the Romans as a
political messiah, his accusers could, super-
ficially, refer to his action in the Temple. But
in reality, by so doing, they distorted and
misrepresented precisely Jesus' real claim. For
he had clearly enough pronounced himself
against any revolt (cf. Mk 12:13-17). Nor was
his action in the Temple to be understood as a
signal for triggering a political uprising. Luke
makes this very clear when he makes Jesus' accusers guilty of distorting his claim into a
political pretension by quoting their very own
words: "We found this man inciting our people
to revolt, opposing payment of the tribute to

Caesar, and claiming to be Christ, a king" (Lk 23:2). Hence the makers of this charge had deliberately set in motion a second proceeding, a political trial in which the central issue at stake was no less than "high treason."

It is Friday morning. When the procurators of Caesarea on the coast came to Jerusalem they customarily took up residence in the old royal palace on the western slope of the Temple mount. This was the site of the Jerusalem praetorium. Seemingly they liked to hold sessions scheduled on the court calendar in the open air in front of the palace. Thus reports Josephus about the later procurator Gessius Florus: "Florus lodged at the palace, and on the following day had a tribunal placed in front of the building and took his seat; the high priests, the nobles, and the most eminent citizens then presented themselves before the tribunal" (*The Jewish War*, Book II, 14-8-301). Pilate no doubt had similarly taken his seat before the praetorium. How does he react to the charge against Jesus? He obviously hesitated simply to yield to it without further ado. All four gospels are in accord on this point. The reason for his hesitation can be specified absolutely.

First of all, as a Roman official, Pilate could not allow himself to be satisfied with vague charges. He was empowered to impose a death sentence only if a capital offense could be proved against Jesus. He required real proof, hard evidence, that Jesus had called for the political overthrow of the regime or had actively participated in disorders. Obviously such a charge could not be proved, and Pilate undoubtedly had perceived that at a glance. And already after his brief confrontation with Jesus, he had probably no longer taken seriously the charge that the accused was a political agitator.

Pilate's refusal to yield to the charge without hesitation, however, could also have had other reasons. As we know from different ancient witnesses, Pilate's attitude toward the Jews was more hostile than friendly. The Jewish philosopher Philo in his book *Legatio ad Gaium* writes about Pilate, among other things: ". . . nor did he wish to do anything which would please his subjects" (38; 303).

Josephus reports an incident characteristic of Pilate's ruthlessness. The procurator had taken money for the construction of an aqueduct to Jerusalem from the Temple's sacred treasury—presumably with the approval of the Jewish leadership:

Indignant at this procedure, the populace formed a ring around the tribunal of Pilate, then on a visit to

Jerusalem, and besieged him with angry clamor. He, foreseeing the tumult, had interspersed among the crowd a troop of his soldiers, armed but disguised in civilian dress, with orders not to use their swords, but to beat any rioters with cudgels. When he gave the agreed signal from his tribunal, large numbers of the Jews perished, some from the blows which they received, others trodden to death by their companions in the ensuing flight. Cowed by the fate of the victims, the multitude was reduced to silence . . . (*The Jewish War*, 9, 4; 175).

A rather clear picture of Pilate's anti-Jewish stance emerges already from the two texts. Therefore, we may assume that he immediately balked when he realized that the Jewish authorities wanted to use him to put a Galilean who was in their disfavor on the cross.

Hence there are perfectly sound reasons that make Pilate's striking efforts to free Jesus quite understandable. To be sure, he could not allow himself simply to free Jesus forthwith and send the accused home. The charge of political agitation was much too serious for that. Pilate therefore, first and foremost, tries to create a basis for an acquittal of Jesus. For this he demands the help of Herod Antipas, tetrarch of Galilee, of which Jesus is a native. Herod, it seems, is also sojourning in Jerusalem for the Passover feast. So Pilate has Jesus delivered to Herod.

7
BEFORE HEROD

The interruption of the Roman trial by the delivery of Jesus to Herod is related only by Luke (23:6-12). There is no supporting evidence whatsoever of this move in Mark, Matthew and John. For this reason the historical worth of the account has been expressly contested and designated as a purely literary construction. This scepticism, however, overlooks the fact that Luke also elsewhere transmits to us from his special narrative fund valuable items of information connected with Herod Antipas (Lk 8:3; 13:31; cf. Acts 13:1).

The undeniable fact that Pilate had hesitated to give in to the pressure of the Council makes a delivery of Jesus to Herod not only possible, but even plausible. Pilate probably knew that Jesus came from Galilee or was so apprised at the trial at the latest. Therefore, he could fetch himself an extrajudicial witness in the matter from whom he could expect a positive deposition in regard to the accused. After all, Herod Antipas up to now had not undertaken any serious action against Jesus, although he had the opportunity to do so for a long time. Such a witness who would confirm the political harmlessness of Jesus the Galilean could then allow Pilate to acquit the accused outwardly as well as inwardly.

Herod does Pilate the expected favor. To be sure, he does it in his own way. First of all, he asks Jesus many inquisitive questions and hopes to see him work a miracle. Jesus can only be silent in the presence of this mixture of curiosity, miracle-mania and superstition. In consequence, the king's mood soon undergoes a radical change. Together with his retinue he makes contemptuous and demeaning mock of Jesus, has a rich cloak thrown over him, and sends him thus attired back to Pilate.

Through the symbolism of this gross performance Pilate is given a signal: The man from Nazareth is a laughable figure; he is politically harmless; he poses no danger to the Roman state. The procurator's own judgment on Jesus' harmlessness must have been confirmed by Herod's behavior. Thus Pilate at the last minute was sufficiently assured, now outwardly as well, that he could acquit Jesus.

8
PILATE'S DEATH SENTENCE

An acquittal does not ensue, however; something quite different transpires. Pilate, in an act of amnesty, offers to release Jesus to the Jews. How can this so surprising a development be explained?

According to the evangelists Matthew, Mark and John, the Roman procurator customarily released a prisoner to the Jews on the day of the Passover festival (Mt 27:15; Mk 15:6; Jn 18:39). Perhaps the Jewish delegation that was to present the amnesty petition had already arrived at the praetorium in the morning. Perhaps it showed up at a later point in time (cf. Mk 15:8). In any event the candidate for amnesty, namely a certain Barabbas, had already been decided for some time. He was being held in prison together with several others who had engaged in an uprising and who had committed a murder at the same time. The "uprising" that had probably taken place shortly before might have been marked by anti-Roman overtones. The striking formulation in Mark (cf. 15:7) suggests that Barabbas was not the chief culprit but an accessory or—formulated more prudently—one of those accused of being an accessory to the crime. The delegation must have consisted above all of friends and relatives of Barabbas.

Pilate surely must have known that in this year he would be petitioned to release Barabbas in the framework of the customary Passover amnesty. It would be naive to assume that Pilate did not yet know the concrete remonstrances of the amnesty delegation. He certainly saw that the release of a man who had been arrested for terrorist activity constituted a high risk that ran strictly counter to his own interests and the interests of Rome. On the other hand, a prisoner had to be released on the Passover feast day; this custom is all too surely attested by the gospels for it to be subject to any doubt whatsoever. In this situation, a perfectly ideal solution that would have imposed itself on the mind of a man like Pilate would be to propose Jesus as a candidate for the Passover amnesty in opposition to the Jewish remonstrances. Such a solution, at first sight, must in every respect appear as an expedient one. In this way Pilate could be relieved of the extremely troublesome "Jesus case" and, at the same time, prevent an amnesty grant to Barabbas. Further, it would absolve him from his official obligation to charge the person of Jesus himself with any wrongdoing.

It is even possible that Pilate's strategy from the outset was oriented toward that aim.

In that case the intention behind handing Jesus over to Herod would not be to prepare an acquittal for the accused, but rather to certify that he was harmless compared with Barabbas, and to insure the possibility of proclaiming an amnesty for Jesus.

Pilate's calculating game is no longer reconstructible with any degree of sureness of all its details. But we may on good grounds proceed from the supposition that his effort to acquit Jesus ultimately ensued from his tactical calculation to prevent the release of the rebel Barabbas whom he viewed as incomparably more dangerous.

Subsequently, however, this very calculation was to prove to be a grave error. Pilate no doubt had all too little reckoned with the possibility that his negotiation partners could stiffen in their support of Barabbas, and he certainly had underestimated by far the energy with which the Jewish authorities would prosecute Jesus' execution. Above all, however, by proposing to release Jesus in the place of Barabbas, he had de facto publicly confirmed Jesus' guilt. His maneuvering had now merely placed him in a situation in which pressure could be brought to bear on him.

Obviously this situation was immediately perceived and exploited by Jesus' enemies. Pilate soon finds himself facing a mass of screaming people, among which organized choruses are loudly clamoring: "Crucify him!" (Mk 15:13f.). The situation had suddenly changed. As the result of his seemingly so clever a strategy, Pilate had let the possibility of a purely judicial decision slip out of his hands.

He had not inquired with judicial impartiality about the guilt or innocence of the accused so that he could base his decision on the information derived from the depositions. Instead, he wanted to make of Jesus an instrument for achieving ulterior aims. From the outset he had mixed the judicial with the political. So it should not be at all surprising that in the end he decides only on the political plane—and, indeed, against Jesus. After all that had preceded this step, Pilate made a full turn around. This is not astonishing when you consider to what degree he had maneuvered politically.

According to John, the determining factor for Pilate's about-face was a hardly concealed Jewish threat to register a complaint about him with the emperor Tiberius: "If you set him free you are no friend of Caesar's; anyone who makes himself king is defying Caesar" (Jn 19:12).

As strange and unbelievable as this kind of talk toward a Roman procurator may sound, historically it cannot be excluded. Tiberius, in particular, was especially sensitive to crimes directed against the *maistas populi Romani*—against the dignity of the Roman people—and by definition also against himself. For Pilate, a Jewish claim with the emperor that Pilate had let a rabble-rouser, who allegedly made claims to royalty while in Roman territory, go unpunished, would have bought grievous consequences in its wake. The way in which Tiberius would have dealt with Pilate is tellingly suggested by an event concerning him that took place several years later and was recorded by Philo.

Pilate had some gold-coated shields brought for dedication purposes into the old Jerusalem royal palace that served him as praetorium

> . . . not so much to honor Tiberius as to annoy the multitude. . . . They had no image work traced on them nor anything else forbidden by the law. Each had only the barest inscription stating two facts, the name of the person who made the dedication and the name of him in whose honor it was made. But when the multitude understood the matter which had by now become a subject of common talk, they, with the king's four sons as

spokesmen, appealed to Pilate to redress the infringement of their traditions caused by the shields and not to disturb the customs which throughout all the preceding ages had been safeguarded without disturbance by kings and by emperors.

When Pilate, who was naturally inflexible, stubbornly refused with a blend of self-will and relentlessness, they clamored, "Do not arouse sedition, do not make war, do not destroy the peace; you do not honor the emperor by dishonoring ancient laws. Do not take Tiberius as your pretext for outraging the nation; he does not wish any of our customs to be overthrown. If you say that he does, produce an order or a letter or something of the kind so that we may cease to pester you and, having chosen our envoys, may petition our lord."

It was this final point which particularly exasperated him, for he feared that if they actually sent an emissary they would also expose the rest of his conduct as governor by stating in full the briberies, the insults, the robberies, the outrages and wanton injuries, the executions without trial constantly repeated, the ceaseless and supremely grievous cruelty. So with all his vindictiveness and furious temper, he was in a difficult position. He had not the courage to take down what had been dedicated nor did he wish to do anything which would please his subjects. At the same time he knew full well the constant policy of Tiberius in these matters.

The magnates saw this and understanding that he had repented of his actions but did not wish to appear penitent, sent letters of very earnest supplication to Tiberius. When Tiberius had read them, what language he used about Pilate, what threats he made! It is needless to describe the violence of his anger, though he was not easily roused to anger, since the facts speak for themselves. For at once without even postponing it to the morrow, he wrote to Pilate with a host of reproaches and rebukes for his audacious violation of precedent and bade him take down the shields at once and have them transferred from the capital to Caesarea on the coast . . . to be set up in the temple of Augustus, and so they were (*Legatio ad Galum*, 38—*The Embassy to Gaius* 38).

Philo's portrayal is in many respects instructive. It shows that Pilate, despite all his outward ruthlessness, nevertheless was fundamentally insecure and wavering. But it also shows the obstinacy with which the Jerusalem populace was accustomed to stand up for its religious views even against Pilate's resistance—even here, incidentally, with clamorous and aggressive catchwords. It also shows further how the Jerusalem protesters knew how to skillfully play off the emperor's policy against the procurator's position and, indeed, through the same threat employed in the case of Jesus. Finally, Philo's portrayal shows how seriously Pilate had to take any denunciations lodged with the emperor.

The Council certainly conducted itself with the same obstinacy and skillfulness in the trial of Jesus. But, in contrast to the incident of the gold-coated shields, here Pilate indeed yielded much more quickly, inwardly and outwardly. He yielded to the pressure that the Council put on him. He gave up his original aim to ensure Barabbas' execution by giving amnesty to Jesus and sentenced Jesus to death on the cross as a political criminal. And, at the same time, he probably pronounced the customary formula: *Ibis in crucem*—"You will ascend the cross."

9
THE EXECUTION

Pilate's strategy, which ended in helplessness and cowardice, signified death for Jesus, a death by one of the cruelest methods of execution ever devised by humans for other humans. With the Romans, the penalty of death on the cross was considered so horrible and dishonorable that it could be decreed only against slaves and non-Romans. From Cicero stems the phrase: "A hangman, a covered head, and the very word 'cross' should remain far not only from the body of Roman citizens, but also from their thoughts, their eyes, their ears" (*Pro Rabiro* 16). Even among slaves and provincials, however, death on the cross was limited to serious crimes such as murder, temple thefts, high treason and insurrection.

According to Roman usage, every crucifixion was preceded by a scourging. Mark and Matthew report on this aspect (Mk 15:15; Mt 27:26). In their accounts, the scourging of Jesus clearly has the function of a punishment initiating the crucifixion and belonging thereto. According to the presentation in the fourth gospel, on the other hand, the scourging of Jesus is carried out already before the death sentence (Jn 19:1; cf. Lk 23:16). In this case, it might have been a last attempt on the part of the procurator to evade passing a death sentence on Jesus. According to this presentation, Pilate must have reckoned that the Council and the crowd of onlookers would be satisfied with Jesus' scourging and renounce their demand for the death penalty.

But regardless of how Jesus' scourging ensues—as a punishment accompanying crucifixion *after* the sentence was pronounced or as the last attempt at placating the excited crowd *before* an eventual death sentence—the fact is, Jesus was scourged by Roman soldiers.

Already before the actual execution, therefore, Jesus had to submit to a punishment so gruesome that it could cause instant death. Josephus relates that as a commander in Galilee he himself had once ordered the scourging of some of his Jewish fellow countrymen, a scourging so lacerating that their entrails were laid bare (*The Jewish War* II, 21, 5; 612 f.). The prophet Jesus, son of Ananias, who since 62 A.D. had prophesied the destruction of the city of Jerusalem and of the Temple, was delivered by the Jewish authorities to the then governing procurator, Albinus, and was flayed to the bone (*The Jewish War* VI, 5, 3; 304). Of the Alexandrian Jews who were scourged at the order of the procurator Flaccus, a part of them died at once from the terrible wounds during the scourging, while others lay sick for a long time, despairing of recovery (Philo, in *Flaccus*, 10; 75). The Roman practice of scourging was so dangerous because the number of blows was not limited and the scourge thongs were often interspersed with pieces of bone or metal. All this gives us an idea of what the brief sentence "So Pilate . . . handed him over to be crucified" in Mark 15:15 means. In addition, after he has been handed over, the Roman soldiers carry on their little game with him. They deck him out as king, imitate the solemn royal proclamations, and kneel before him in homage (Mk 15:16-20). Thus they continue exactly what had already been begun by Herod's courtiers. To be sure, they do it as soldiers of a legion; the "Hail, King of the Jews!" is accompanied by brutal blows in the face (Jn 19:3; Mk 15:19). Because of the scourging and the accompanying mockery Jesus is no longer in condition to carry the cross to the execution site by himself. Therefore, the soldiers force a certain Simon of Cyrene, who is just coming from working in the field and who meets the execution squad by chance, to carry Jesus' cross (Mk 15:21).

One should not imagine this cross-bearing as it is depicted in countless Christian presentations. At regular executions the condemned did not carry the whole cross, but only the cross beam. Stakes driven firmly and, in most cases permanently, in the ground served as upright beams. Upon arrival at the place of execution, the condemned was laid flat on the ground, nailed with arms outstretched on the transom, and together with it elevated to the upright beam. The transom was made fast on top and only then were the feet nailed to the wood. Thus Jesus and Simon of Cyrene did not carry the whole cross, but only the cross beam. That Jesus could not even carry this one beam shows that after the scourging he was already at the end of his strength.

En route to the place of execution, the condemned also carried an inscription (*titulus*) stating the reason for the condemnation fixed to the beam. In Jesus' case the *titulus* read:

> *Jesus of Nazareth*
> *The King of the Jews*
> (Jn 19:19; cf. Mk 15:26)

The fact that Pilate wrote on the placard "The King of the Jews" and not "He passed himself off as King of the Jews" can be understood only as a mockery of the Jews. Obviously, after coming out on the losing end in the bout with the Council, Pilate wanted to recover his losses at least in this form. At the same time, in the formulation of the *titulus*

there also lies a spiteful irony against Jesus.
Now, after Herod and his retinue had mocked
Jesus and the Roman soldiers had played their
rough little game with him, the mockery con-
tinues.

Moreover, the gospel account that Jesus
was crucified between two rebels is consistent
with the sustained mockery symbolism. A
king cannot appear without a royal council.
He must have it beside him on the occasion of
his solemn public appearances. The royal
council that is carefully posted "to the right"
and "to the left" of Jesus (cf. Mk 15:27) con-
sists of two agitators. Jesus is enthroned in the
middle.

The hill on which Jesus was executed bore
the name Golgotha, which means simply
"place of the skull" (Mk 15:22; Jn 19:17). It
was so called not because the skulls of earlier
executions lay around the site—that would
have been unthinkable in view of the Jewish
burial customs—but because the hill had the
form of a skull. The Church of the Holy
Sepulchre now occupies the site where Jesus
died. As probings conducted in the area in
1961 showed, it had been the site of a stone
quarry abandoned since the time of the
Israelite monarchy. Private tombs were hewn
in the rocky heights to the west on the terrain
of this former quarry. To the east, in the direc-

tion of the city, there rose a still extant mass of rock—"the skull"—around which were gardens (cf. Jn 19:41; 20:15). This also clearly suggests that we must imagine the Golgotha rock and its environs as lying outside the city walls of that time. To be sure, only a narrow hollow lay between Golgotha and the west wall of Jerusalem. Jesus' way of the cross from the praetorium to the city wall and from there to the place of execution was not very far, assuming, of course, that the shortest way had been taken.

According to Mark, the execution squad arrived in the course of the morning at Golgotha, at the third hour, that is, around 9 a.m. There they nailed Jesus to the cross. The crucifixion with its dreadful suffering is not described in the gospels. Tact and artistic taste prohibited the primitive church from so doing. With extreme brevity and dispassion, Mark writes only the three words at the end of the sentence: ". . . they crucified him" (15:24).

Immediately before the crucifixion Jesus was offered wine mixed with myrrh (Mk 15:23). This was a narcotic drink which, according to Jewish custom, was to be proffered to the condemned before their execution: "To him, who was on the way to be executed, was given a tiny piece of frankincense in a cup of wine in order to numb his senses" (Babylonian

Talmud, in the tract *Sanhedrin* 43-a). Thus the wine spiked with strong condiment was supposed to make the torments of execution more endurable. Jesus, however, refused the wine.

Jesus' action here is to be distinguished from an incident that transpires only later when he hangs on the cross in the throes of death. At this point one of the bystanders tries to give Jesus a drink by soaking a sponge in vinegar and fixing it to the end of a reed which he holds in front of Jesus' mouth (Mk 15:36). It can no longer be determined whether the bystander does this out of pity or whether he merely wants to refresh Jesus in order to prolong the death agony. The incident, however, clearly shows that Jesus was on a high cross; the upright beam must have been long and sturdy and certainly firmly and permanently anchored in the ground.

After Jesus was nailed to the cross, the soldiers shared his clothing among themselves (Mk 15:24). The members of an execution squad had the unwritten right to take whatever a victim of an execution wore on his body. In Jesus' case it involved the outer and undergarments, the girdle, sandals and perhaps also a headband.

While Jesus hung on the cross he was mocked and taunted by the passersby—the city wall was not too far away—and by the bystanders who turned up at the execution site. As at the palace of Herod Antipas and in the praetorium, the mocking related above all to his confession as the Christ that is summed up in the *titulus*, "The King of the Jews." Thus, for example, it was said: "Let the Christ, the King of Israel, come down from the cross now, for us to see it and believe" (Mk 15:32). The background of this taunt is the belief that Jesus' crucifixion presented the palpable refutation of his claim. The true Christ would never hang on a cross and suffer but, on the contrary, crush and annihilate his enemies.

According to Mark, Jesus, at the ninth hour or about 3 p.m., prayerfully recited in a loud voice the beginning of the 22nd Psalm: "My God, my God, why have you deserted me?" This prayerful cry is misunderstood by some of the bystanders as a call to Elijah: "Listen, he is calling on Elijah." Thereupon followed the attempt mentioned above to give Jesus vinegar to drink. But at that very moment Jesus gave out a loud cry and breathed his last (Mk 15:34-37).

What Jesus' last word actually was is still disputed by exegetes up to our day. For it is only in Mark and Matthew that Jesus prayerfully recites the beginning of the 22nd Psalm before his death. In Luke, instead, he calls: "Father, into your hands I commit my spirit"

(Lk 23:46), thereby citing Psalm 31:5. In John, finally, Jesus' last word is: "It is accomplished" (Jn 19:30). Despite this divergence of the textual tradition, a reconstruction of Jesus' last word is possible.

In this connection, the fourth gospel can be disregarded. It goes its own way and tries with the words, "It is accomplished," to interpret the whole of Jesus' salvific action theologically. But Jesus' last word in Luke is also secondary. It clearly corresponds with the Lukan theology (cf. Acts 7:59).

Mark is the real point of departure. He can only base himself on a very old tradition of the primitive community since he renders Psalm 22:1 in Aramaic: *Eloi, Eloi, lema sabachthani!* To be sure, it is precisely the Aramaic word *Eloi* ("my God") that creates real difficulties for the exegete. For phonetically this word hardly lends itself to being misunderstood as a call to the Jewish helper in need, Elijah. Moreover, the claim that the primitive community was the first to put the beginning words of the 22nd Psalm in Jesus' mouth because it used this psalm at a very early date for the interpretation of the whole passion is not satisfactory. For then the misunderstanding, "Listen, he is calling Elijah," would also have to be a secondary construction of an early Christian narrator. But that is wholly improbable. What is much more probable is that Psalm 22 plays so decisive a role very early for the theological interpretation of Jesus' death solely for the reason that Jesus actually uttered this prayer on the cross. And the Elijah misunderstanding must have been occasioned precisely through Psalm 22. But how?

The simplest solution to offer itself is that Jesus had prayed brief bits or fragments of particular sentences of the psalm in Hebrew. He could no longer have been physically capable of reciting the whole psalm in a loud voice. One of these fragments was the shattering beginning of the psalm: "My God, my God, why have you deserted me?" This sentence corresponded exactly to Jesus' abandonment and gruesome death agony. In a later passage in the 22nd Psalm, we then come upon the prayerful call: *Eli atta*—"You have been my God!" (22:10). Perhaps precisely this utterance was Jesus' last cry of which Mark 15:37 reports. At any rate, with the call *Eli atta* the misunderstanding, "He is calling on Elijah," would be really plausible. For the Hebrew *Eli atta*, phonetically, could easily be misunderstood as an Aramaic *Elijja ta* — "Elijah, come!"

The fact that Jesus died with fragments of the 22nd Psalm on his lips would suggest that his life did not end in despair but, despite the endless agony, in an unfathomable trust in God: "You are my God—in spite of everything!"

It is astonishing that Jesus expired after only six hours on the cross. In most cases, the death agony of the crucified lasted much longer. The inhuman cruelty of execution on the cross consisted precisely in the fact that it aimed at a very slow, repeatedly postponed death. In most cases, the failure of the blood to circulate was the actual cause of death. The moment his strength was no more, the crucified person hung from the arms with the full weight of his body. This in a short space of time inevitably led to serious disturbances occasioned by blood loss and an oppressive asthma. Hence the victim involuntarily drew himself up, placing more weight on the foot wounds. The moment he collapsed anew from exhaustion, the horrendous sequence of collapsing and drawing himself up began all over again. Precisely because the feet were nailed, and thus for a time could shore up the body, the agony of the crucified—depending on the kind of nailing and whether a supporting peg had been used—could be prolonged for days.

If it was desired that the crucified died quickly, their tibias were broken. In that case, the body weight hung even more heavily from the arms, and death ensued quickly through circulatory failure. A surprising find of the remains of a crucified victim from the Hellenist-Roman world, the very first discovery of its kind, was made in Jerusalem in 1968. The archeologists found not only a rusty nail that had pierced through both feet joined together, but also both shinbones broken at the same height as the result of powerful blows. Thus the usage of *crucifragium* reported by John (Jn 19:32) is also archeologically confirmed.

According to John, the deaths of the two rebels who were crucified with Jesus were hastened by breaking their legs. On the other hand, Jesus' legs were not broken, since he was already dead. That Jesus expired after six hours must have been occasioned by the cruel scourging and the consequent loss of blood.

10
THE BURIAL

In the ancient world the penalty of crucifixion in general was sharpened further by refusing the victim a grave. This meant that the corpses of the crucified remained hanging on the cross until they were torn to pieces by birds of prey and wild beasts. Only then were the remains buried somewhere.

For the ancients a refusal of burial was much more terrible than it is for us. In this way the executed were further desecrated. They were stripped of the funeral honors and their "afterlife" was shattered forevermore.

For the Jewish sensibility, the refusal of the grave was not only a dreadful dishonoring of the dead, but beyond that a cultic defilement of the land. There was such an anxious concern for the proper observance of the burial rite that even enemies and executed criminals were scrupulously laid to rest. For this reason, the burial custom even in ancient Israel required that the length of time the condemned was to hang from a stake, even after being pronounced dead, be limited to the evening of the day of execution.

"If a man guilty of a capital offense is put to death and you hang him on a tree, his body must not remain on the tree overnight; you must bury him the same day, for one who has been hanged is accursed of God, and you must not defile the land that Yahweh your God gives you for an inheritance" (Dt 21:22 f.).

This text from the book of Deuteronomy was extended to the crucified in the rabbinical exegesis. Victims of crucifixion also were not to remain hanging on the cross overnight, but were to be taken down and buried before sundown.

Thus it becomes understandable that, according to the fourth gospel, delegates of the Council should ask that the deaths of the three crucified be hastened by breaking their legs (Jn 19:31). Only thus could their corpses be buried at the right time. That the following day was a Sabbath made it all the more urgent, in the view of the Jewish authorities, that the execution be ended by late afternoon. It may also be assumed that the Council wanted to assure itself that Jesus was properly dead.

Parallel to this action or in conjunction with it, a prominent member of the Council, Joseph of Arimathaea, personally addressed a petition to Pilate for the release of the body of Jesus. Whether this Joseph actually was a Council member or whether he belonged to the delegation of the Council which petitioned for the quick death of the crucified trio must re-

main an open question. In any case, he was a
Jesus sympathizer. And he was a man who
possessed sufficient esteem as to venture to ad-
dress a petition to the Roman procurator.
Pilate granted his request, but only after he
was assured of Jesus' death by a member of the
execution squad (Mk 15:42-45).

Thereafter, everything proceeded very
swiftly. Joseph of Arimathaea attended to the
purchase of a shroud. Jesus' corpse was taken
down from the cross. Then Jesus was wrapped
in the newly bought shroud and was laid to
rest in a tomb. Women who belonged to Jesus'
circle of disciples were present at the scene.

On the basis of many archeological
parallels in and near Jerusalem and on the
basis of the accounts in all four gospels, we can
construct for ourselves a very concrete image
of Jesus' tomb. It lay near the Golgotha rocks
(Jn 19:41); it was hewn into one of the rock
ledges which traversed the abandoned quarry
west of Golgotha (Jn 19:41); it was a
sepulchral chamber with burial benches on the
sides. The entrance was relatively low,
through which one could enter only in a
stooped position, and it was closed with a
large stone (Mk 15:46). Finally, it was a hither-
to unused grave (Mt 27:60; Lk 23:53; Jn
19:41).

Hence on the basis of these considerations

it can be safely asserted that the body of Jesus did not remain on the cross, nor was it buried in a common grave for criminals but, rather, he was interred in a family tomb, the site of which was known in Jerusalem. On the morning of the first weekday after the Sabbath, the women went to this tomb. But that is another story. . . .

AFTERWORD

The events of the passion were compressed in the span of a few hours. The arrest, the proceedings of the Council, the delivery to Pilate, the hearing, the delivery to Herod, the scourging, the mocking, the execution—all that transpired in one night and a day. Those who wanted Jesus' death knew very well why everything had to proceed so quickly. And they very well understood how to go about their business.

The strategies employed by Jesus' enemies also belong to this business. The Council, of course, condemned Jesus within the framework of Jewish law. But before Pilate it made of the "seducer of the people" a political agitator, and from Jesus' confession it deduced an avowal that he was a messiah with political intentions. It was exactly this strategy that fully distorted Jesus' claim and that in the end proved to be fatal for him.

But Pilate also pursued his strategies. He wanted to prevent the release of Barabbas in virtue of the Passover custom. Thus Jesus became a means to an end. Pilate was so entangled in the execution of his strategy that he failed to notice how, by proposing an amnesty for Jesus in the place of Barabbas, he had already pronounced Jesus guilty and thus allowed the juridical possibilities still open to him to slip out of his hand. Thus Pilate's political strategy proved just as fatal for Jesus.

To be sure, Pilate, despite his much greater power, was the weaker figure in this game of crisscrossing strategies. In complete contrast to Pilate, the Council never lost control but pursued its aim imperturbably. Its aim was to hang Jesus from a cross. The perseverance of the Jewish authorities in seeking this purpose can hardly be understood without bearing in mind the background of Deuteronomy 21, 22 f.: *For one who has been hanged is accursed of God.* If crucifixion already for the ancient world was the most ignominious and dishonorable death imaginable, it had an even more symbolic power for Jewish theology on the basis of this text. And, according to Jewish Law, it is precisely religious seducers of the people who must be hung on the tree so that their teaching and practice be publicly exposed. Viewed in this light, for the Council, although the Passover feast with its masses of pilgrims made an arrest of Jesus carried out by the police disagreeably more difficult, it had the positive effect of providing an opportunity to expose Jesus publicly before the gathering of Israel as one accursed of God. For once Jesus hung on the cross, one thing was obvious: God in no way could stay behind such a man.

All these strategies show that Jesus fell between the millstones of powers that were much stronger than he—powers that either did not desire a dialogue on the question of truth or felt bound to render Jesus harmless in virtue of their religious duty. Here it is alarming to see how groups in Judaism who otherwise fought bitterly among themselves suddenly form a united front in the case of Jesus. Most surprisingly, for once Pharisees and Sadducees have exactly the same aim. Pilate and Herod Antipas, who up to then were hostile to one another, also become friends on that day (Lk 23:12). Jesus has nothing to say to them; therefore he is silent.

What is also striking for the observer of the passion events is the hatred that is repeatedly vented on Jesus. It is shown in the painful scene before the Council, it is expressed in the mockery of Jesus by Herod and his retinue, it crops up again in the mockery of Jesus by the Roman cohorts, and it shows itself once more in the taunts of the bystanders at Golgotha.

This excess of scorn has led many exegetes to the opinion that all the mockery scenes should, in the light of "tradition-history" and therefore historically, be reduced to a single scene, the mockery of Jesus by the Roman soldiers. But this argument overlooks the fact that the reality is much more complex than the smooth and unilateral constructions of theorists. Further, it overlooks the power of mimicry: namely, that evil, once it happens, is imitated—and indeed often in a primitive and slavish manner. Finally, it overlooks what Plato already knew—that a man who is wholly just and good becomes intolerable in the eyes of those who do not want to decide for the good. They necessarily harbor a deadly hate for him (*The Republic* 361e-362a).

What has been discussed up to now, as we stated in the Introduction, should not be naively simplified in the manner of a passion play: here the holy; there the wicked! From the outset it was stressed that the Pharisees and the Sadducees, in the final analysis, acted according to their religious conscience. The abyssal nature of their conflict with Jesus results primarily from the fact that here it is not simply a question of evil against good. Rather, it is one of men who want to defend the honor of God and the law of God against an action that, according to their opinion, blasphemes the honor of God and destroys the holy Law.

It must also be noted that in the conflict between Jesus and his enemies charisma and institutions clash. The Council defends Temple and Torah in the name of God against one who, in the name of God, calls into question Temple and Torah, because he proclaims a still deeper bond of God to humanity than was possible through the Temple and the Law.

We can go one more step further still and show that ultimately it is the tension between law and gospel that stands behind the whole conflict. It is precisely this insight that makes it clear that the question regarding the guilt of Jesus' enemies is much more complicated than it seems to be at first. For, after all, it involves a conflict in which we are all involved and in which we repeatedly make ourselves guilty; we, too, constantly pay no attention to God's true claim that comes from the gospel, we deck it out with our own institutions and laws and thus minimize it.

Hence an inquiry into the immediate background of the passion events cannot be concerned with mitigating or leveling the guilt of Jesus' enemies. On the contrary, its aim must be to expose this guilt in its depth, for precisely by so doing will all of our own guilt be exposed.

As a reader of the passion history, therefore, I should repeatedly ask myself with which protagonist of the narrative I identify. If I identify only with Jesus and completely remove myself from his adversaries, I have still not perceived the abyssal nature of the conflict that is related there. Only in the moment when I discern that I myself, ever and anew, play exactly the same role that was played by the Council or Pilate at that time, will I have grasped what the passion is really all about.

BIBLIOGRAPHY

The preceding presentation is gratefully based on the research findings of exegetes who have worked as specialists on the theme of the passion of Jesus. The works involved are listed in the bibliography below. Three of them were repeatedly drawn on: the great work by J. Blinzler, *Der Prozess Jesu (The Trial of Jesus)*, the highly instructive investigation by A. Strobel, *Die Stunde der Wahrheit (The Hour of Truth)*, and the path-breaking Mark commentary by R. Pesch.

Blinzler, J. *Der Prozess Jesu*, Regensburg 1969.

Bajsic, A. *Pilatus, Jesus und Barabbas*, in *Biblica* 48 (1967) 7-28.

Boman, T. *Das letze Wort Jesu*, in *Studia theologica* 17 (1963) 103-119.

Gese, H. *Psalm 22 und das Neue Testament*, in the collection, *Vom Sinai zum Zion* (Beiträge zur Evangelischen Theologie 64), Munich 1974, 180-201.

Hengel, M. *Mors turpissima crucis. Die Kreuzigung in der antiken Welt* and the "Torheit" of "Wortes vom Kreuz," in Friedrich, J.-Pöhlmann, W.-Stuhlmacher, P. (Editors), *Rechtfertigung. Festschrift für Ernst*

Käsemann zum 70. Geburtstag, Tübingen 1976, 125-184.

Müller, K. *Jesus und die Sadduzäer,* in Merklein, H.-Lange, J. (Editors), *Biblische Randbemerkungen. Schulerfestschrift für* Rudolf Schnackenburg zum 60. Geburtstag, Würzburg 1974, 3-24.

Pesch, R., *Das Markusevangelium,* Part II (*Herders Theologischer Kommentar zum Neuen Testament* II 2), Freiburg i. Br. 1977.

Schnackenburg, R., *Das Evangelium nach Markus,* 2. Part (Geistliche Schriftlesung 2/2), Düsseldorf 1971.

Strobel, A. *Die Stunde der Wahrheit. Untersuchungen zum Strafverfahren gegen Jesus* (*Wissenschaftliche Untersuchungen zum Neuen Testament* 21), Tübingen 1980.